# The New :01 One Minute Manager

## ALSO BY KEN BLANCHARD, PhD

THE ONE MINUTE MANAGER (with Spencer Johnson)

PUTTING THE ONE MINUTE MANAGER TO WORK
(with Robert Lorber)

LEADERSHIP AND THE ONE MINUTE MANAGER
(with Pat Zigarmi and Drea Zigarmi)

THE ONE MINUTE MANAGER MEETS THE MONKEY
(with William Oncken)

THE ONE MINUTE MANAGER BUILDS HIGH PERFORMING
TEAMS (with Don Carew and Eunice Parisi-Carew)

RAVING FANS (with Sheldon Bowles)

GUNG HO! (with Sheldon Bowles)

HIGH FIVE! (with Sheldon Bowles, Don Carew, and
Eunice Parisi-Carew)

WHALE DONE! (with Thad Lacinak, Chuck Tompkins,
and Jim Ballard)

FULL STEAM AHEAD! (with Jesse Stoner)

THE SECRET (with Mark Miller)

THE ONE MINUTE FATHER The Quickest Way For Fathers To Help Children Like Themselves And Behave Themselves

THE ONE MINUTE TEACHER How To Teach Others To Teach Themselves (with Constance Johnson, MEd)

THE PRECIOUS PRESENT The Gift You Give Yourself

ONE MINUTE FOR YOURSELF Taking Care Of Your Most Valuable Asset

THE VALUE TALES SERIES FOR CHILDREN

# The New :01 One Minute Manager®

## Ken Blanchard, PhD

## Spencer Johnson, MD

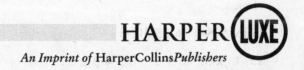
An Imprint of HarperCollinsPublishers

THE NEW ONE MINUTE MANAGER. Copyright © 2015 by Blanchard Family Partnership and Candle Communications, Inc. All rights reserved. Printed in the United States of America. No part of this book may be used or reproduced in any manner whatsoever without written permission except in the case of brief quotations embodied in critical articles and reviews. For information address HarperCollins Publishers, 195 Broadway, New York, NY 10007.

HarperCollins books may be purchased for educational, business, or sales promotional use. For information please e-mail the Special Markets Department at SPsales@harpercollins.com.

FIRST HARPERLUXE EDITION

HarperLuxe™ is a trademark of HarperCollins Publishers

Library of Congress Cataloging-in-Publication Data is available upon request.

ISBN: 978-0-06-239312-8

15 ID/RRD 10 9 8 7 6 5 4 3 2

*The Symbol*

The New One Minute Manager's symbol is intended to remind each of us to take a minute out of our day to look into the faces of the people we lead and manage. And to realize that they are our most important resources.

# The New One Minute Manager

# Table of Contents

A Message from the Authors      xv

The Story of The New One Minute Manager

The Search      1

The New One Minute Manager      7

The First Secret: One Minute Goals      14

One Minute Goals: Summary      23

The Second Secret: One Minute Praisings      25

One Minute Praisings: Summary      33

The Appraisal      36

The Third Secret: One Minute Re-Directs      38

One Minute Re-Directs: Summary      47

The New One Minute Manager Explains      49

Why One Minute Goals Work      53

Why One Minute Praisings Work      64

Why One Minute Re-Directs Work    71

Another New One Minute Manager    86

The New One Minute Manager's Game Plan    88

A Gift to Yourself    89

A Gift to Others    92

Acknowledgments    95

About the Authors    97

Take the Next Step    100

# A Message from the Authors

The world has changed since the publication of the original *One Minute Manager*. Today, organizations must respond faster, with fewer resources, to keep up with ever-changing technology and globalization.

To help you lead, manage, and succeed in this changing world, we're happy to offer you *The New One Minute Manager*.

Since the underlying principles in the now-classic story remain the same—and have helped so many millions of people around the world—a good deal of this story also remains the same.

But, just as the world has changed, so has the One Minute Manager. He has a *new*, more collaborative approach to leading and motivating people.

When he first started teaching his Three Secrets, top-down leadership was a way of life.

These days effective leadership is more of a side-by-side relationship. You'll see that reflected in *The New One Minute Manager.*

Today, people look for more fulfillment in their work and their lives. They want to feel engaged and make a meaningful contribution. They're less willing to trade time on the job to satisfy needs outside of work.

The New One Minute Manager understands this, and treats people accordingly—knowing they are key contributors to the organization's success. He realizes that attracting and keeping talent is a top priority.

The key is how he *uses* his new approach.

As the ancient sage Confucius advises, "The essence of knowledge is, having it, to use it."

We trust you'll consider using the Three Secrets you'll discover in *The New One Minute Manager* to succeed in your changing world—not only with colleagues and associates at work, but also with your family and friends.

If you do, we're confident that you and the people you work and live with will enjoy healthier, happier, and more productive lives.

Ken Blanchard, PhD
Spencer Johnson, MD

# The New One Minute Manager

O nce there was a bright young man who was looking for a special kind of manager who could lead
and manage in today's changing world.

He wanted to find one who encouraged people to
balance their work and their life, so that each became
more meaningful and enjoyable.

He wanted to work for one and he wanted to become
one.

His search had taken him over many years to the far
corners of the world.

He had been in small towns and in the capitals of
powerful nations.

He had spoken with many managers who were trying to deal with a rapidly changing world: executives and entrepreneurs, government administrators and military personnel, university presidents and foundation directors; with managers of shops and stores, of restaurants, banks, and hotels; with men and women— young and old.

He had gone into every kind of office, large and small, luxurious and sparse, with windows and without.

He was beginning to see the full spectrum of how people manage people.

But he wasn't always pleased with what he saw.

He had seen many "tough" managers whose organizations seemed to win while the people working there lost.

Some thought they were good managers. Many thought otherwise.

As the young man sat in each of these "tough" people's offices, he asked, "What kind of a manager would you say you are?"

Their answers varied only slightly.

"I'm a bottom-line manager—I keep on top of the situation," he was told. "Hard-nosed." "Realistic." "Profit-minded."

They said they had always managed that way and saw no reason to change.

He heard the pride in their voices and their interest in results.

The young man also met many "nice" managers whose people seemed to win while their organizations lost.

Some of the people who reported to them thought they were good managers.

Those to whom they reported had their doubts.

As the young man sat and listened to these "nice" people answer the same question, he heard:

"I'm a participative manager." "Supportive." "Considerate." "Humanistic."

They also said they had always managed that way and saw no reason to change.

He heard the pride in their voices and their interest in people.

But he was disturbed.

It was as though most managers in the world were still managing the way they had always done and were primarily interested either in results or in people.

Managers who were interested in results often seemed to be labeled "autocratic," while the ones interested in people were often labeled "democratic."

The young man thought each of these types—the "tough" autocrat and the "nice" democrat—was only partially effective. *It's like being half a manager,* he thought.

He returned home tired and discouraged.

He might have given up his search long ago, but he had one great advantage. He knew exactly what he was looking for.

*In these changing times,* he thought, *the most effective managers manage themselves and the people they work with so that* both *the people and the organization profit from their presence.*

The young man had looked everywhere for an effective manager but had found only a few. The few he did find would not share their secrets with him. He began to think maybe he would never find what he was looking for.

Then he began hearing marvelous stories about a special manager who lived, surprisingly, in a nearby town. He heard that people liked to work for this man and that they produced great results together.

He also heard that when people applied the manager's principles to their personal lives, they got great results as well.

He wondered if the stories were really true and, if so, whether this person would be willing to share his secrets with him.

Curious, he phoned the assistant to this special manager to see if he might get an appointment. To his surprise, the assistant put him through to the manager immediately.

The young man asked when he might be able to meet with him, and the manager said, "Anytime this week is fine, except Wednesday morning. You pick the time."

The young man was puzzled. What kind of manager had that kind of time available? But he was fascinated as well, and went to see him.

When the young man arrived at the Manager's office, he found him looking out the window. The Manager turned and invited him to sit down. "What can I do for you?"

"I've heard great things about you and would like to know more about the way you manage."

"Well, we're using our proven methods in several *new* ways to deal with all the changes that are happening, but we can get to that later. Let's begin with the basics.

"We used to be a top-down managed company, which worked in its time. But today that structure is too slow. It doesn't inspire people and it stifles innovation. Customers demand quicker service and better products, so we need everyone to contribute their talent. The brainpower isn't only in the executive office—it can be found throughout the organization.

"Since speed is a currency of success now, leading with collaboration is far more effective than the old command-and-control system."

"How do you lead with collaboration?"

"I meet with our team once a week on Wednesday mornings—that's why I couldn't meet with you then. At those meetings I listen as our group reviews and analyzes what they achieved the previous week, the problems they had, what remains to be accomplished, and their plans and strategies to get those things done."

"Are the decisions made at those meetings binding on both you and your team?"

"Yes, they are. The purpose of the meeting is for people to participate in making key decisions about what they're going to do next."

"Then you're a participative manager, aren't you?" asked the young man.

"Not really. I believe in facilitating, but not in participating in making other people's decisions."

"Then what is the purpose of your meetings?"

"Didn't I just tell you that?"

The young man felt uncomfortable and wished he hadn't made that mistake.

The Manager paused and took a breath. "We're here to get results. By drawing on the talents of everyone, we're a lot more productive."

"Oh, so you're more results oriented than people-oriented."

The Manager got to his feet and began to walk about. "To succeed sooner, managers must be both results-oriented and people-oriented.

"How on earth can we get results if it's not through people? So I care about people *and* results, because they go hand in hand.

"Take a look at this." The Manager pointed to his computer. "I keep this as my screen saver to remind me of a practical truth."

*

*People Who Feel
Good About
Themselves
Produce
Good Results.*

*

As the young man looked at the screen, the Manager said, "Think about yourself. When do you work best? Is it when you feel good about yourself? Or when you don't?"

The young man nodded as he began to see the obvious. "I get more done when I'm feeling good about myself."

"Of course you do, and so does everyone else."

"So," the visitor said, "helping people feel good about themselves is a key to productivity."

"Yes. However, remember—productivity is more than just the *quantity* of work done. It is also the *quality*." He walked over to the window and said, "Look at this."

When the young man reached the window, the Manager pointed to a restaurant below. "Do you see how many customers that restaurant has?"

The young man saw people lined up outside the restaurant door. "Must be a good location for a restaurant," he observed.

The Manager asked, "If that's true, why aren't people lined up in front of the other restaurant two doors away? Why do people want to eat at the first restaurant and not at the second?"

The young man replied, "Because the food and service are better?"

"Yes. It's pretty simple. Without giving people a quality product and the service they want, you won't stay in business for long.

"It's easy to miss the obvious. The best way to achieve these successful results is with *people*! It's the *people* in the best restaurants that are creating their success."

This piqued the young man's interest. As they sat back down, he said, "You've already stated that you're not a participative manager. Just how would you describe yourself?"

"They call me a New One Minute Manager."

The young man's face showed surprise. "A what?"

The Manager laughed and said, "They call me that because we're finding new ways to get great results in very little time."

Although the young man had spoken with many managers, he had never heard one talk like this. It was hard to believe—someone who gets good results without taking a lot of time.

Seeing the doubt on the young man's face, the Manager said, "You don't believe it, do you?"

"I must admit it's hard for me even to imagine."

The Manager laughed and said, "Listen, if you really want to know what kind of manager I am, why don't you talk with some of the people on our team?"

The Manager turned to his computer, printed out a list, and gave it to the young man. "Those are the names, positions, and phone numbers of the six people who report to me."

"Which ones should I talk to?" the young man asked.

"That's your decision. Pick any name. Talk to any one of them or all of them."

"Well, I mean, who should I start with?"

"As I said earlier, I don't make decisions for other people," the Manager said firmly. "Make that decision yourself." Then he was quiet for what seemed like a long moment.

The young man started to feel uncomfortable, and wished he hadn't asked the Manager to make a decision for him that he could've made himself.

The Manager stood up and walked his visitor to the door. "You want to know about leading and managing people, and I admire that.

"If you have any questions after talking with some of the people on our team," he added, "come back and see me.

"I would, in fact, like to give you the concept of One Minute Management as a gift. Someone gave it to me once and it's made a big difference. When you come to understand it, you may want to become a manager yourself someday."

"Thank you," the young man said.

As he left the office, he passed Courtney, the Manager's assistant.

She said, "I can see from your thoughtful expression that you've already experienced our Manager."

The young man, still trying to figure things out, said, "I guess I have."

"Is there any way I can help you?" she asked.

"Yes, there is. He gave me this list of people I might talk to."

She looked at the list. "Three of these people are traveling this week. However, Teresa Lee, Paul Trenell, and Jon Levy are here today. I'll phone ahead and help you get in to see them."

"I'd appreciate it," said the young man.

When the young man arrived at Teresa Lee's office, she removed her reading glasses and smiled. "I hear you've been to see our Manager. He's quite a guy, isn't he?"

"He seems to be."

"Did he suggest you talk with us about the way he manages?"

"He sure did."

Teresa said, "It's amazing how well it works. I'm still surprised at how little time he needs to spend with me since I've learned how to do my job."

"Is that true?"

"You'd better believe it is. I hardly ever see him now."

"You mean you don't get any help from him?" asked the young man.

"Not as much as I did when I started. Although he does spend time with me at the beginning of a new task or responsibility. That's when he and I set our One Minute Goals."

"One Minute Goals? What are they?"

"That's the first of the Three Secrets to One Minute Management," Teresa said.

"Three Secrets?" the young man asked, wanting to know more.

"Yes," said Teresa. "Setting One Minute Goals is the beginning of One Minute Management. You see, in most organizations when you ask people what they do and then ask their boss, all too often you get two different answers.

"In fact, in some organizations I've worked in, any relationship between what I thought my job responsibilities were and what my boss thought they were was purely coincidental. And then I would get in trouble for not doing something I didn't even think was my job."

"Does that ever happen here?" asked the young man.

"No!" Teresa said. "It doesn't happen here. Our Manager works with us to make it clear what our responsibilities are and what we are being held accountable for."

"Just how does he do that?" the young man wanted to know.

"More efficiently than ever," Teresa said with a smile. "In fact, these days I call him the *New* One Minute Manager, because he's doing things in new ways that are even more effective now."

"How so?"

She explained, "For example, instead of setting our goals for us, he listens to our input and works side-by-side with us to develop them. After we agree on our most important goals, each is described on one page.

"He feels that a goal and its performance standard—what needs to be done and by what due date—should take no more than a paragraph or two to express, so it can be read and reviewed in about a minute.

"Once we've written the goals out concisely, it's easy to look at them often and stay focused on what's important.

"Finally, I e-mail my goals to him and keep copies, so everything is clear and we can both periodically check my progress."

"If you have a one-page description for every goal, wouldn't there be a lot of pages for each person?"

"No, there really aren't. We believe in the 80/20 rule. That is, 80% of your really important results will come from 20% of your goals. So we set One Minute Goals on only that 20%—that is, our key areas of responsibility—maybe three to five goals. Of course, in the event a special project comes up, we set special One Minute Goals."

She continued, "Since each goal can be read in about a minute, we are encouraged to take a moment every now and then to look at what we're doing and see if it matches our goals.

"If not, we adjust what we're doing. It helps us succeed sooner."

The young man observed, "So *you* look to see if you're doing what's expected, rather than waiting for your manager to tell you."

"Yes."

"So, in a way, you're managing yourself."

"Exactly," Teresa said with a nod.

"And it's easier," she added, "because we know what our job is. Our Manager makes sure we know what good performance looks like because he shows us. In other words, expectations are clear to both of us.

"However, many of us work remotely, and our Manager isn't always able to show us in person, but he does so in other ways."

"Can you give me an example?"

"Sure," said Teresa. "One of my goals was to identify a problem and come up with a solution that, when implemented, would turn the situation around.

"Early on, when I started to work here, I was traveling and spotted a problem that needed to be solved, but I didn't know what to do. So I called him. When he answered the phone, I said, 'I have a problem.' Before I could get another word out, he said, 'Good! That's what you've been hired to solve.' Then there was dead silence on the other end of the phone.

"I didn't know what to say. I eventually sputtered, 'But, but . . . I don't know how to solve this problem.'

" 'Teresa,' he said, 'one of your goals for the future is for you to identify and solve your own problems. But since you are new, let's talk. So tell me what the problem is.'

"I then tried to describe the problem the best I could. But I was all over the place, feeling nervous and defensive.

"My Manager put me at ease when he gently said, 'Just tell me what people are doing, or not doing, that's causing the problem.'

"Hearing that made me think about the real problem instead of myself and I described the problem the way he asked me to.

"He said, 'That's good, Teresa! Now tell me what you would like to be happening.'

" 'I'm not sure I know,' I said.

" 'Then call me back when you know,' he said.

"I just froze in amazement for a few seconds. I didn't know what to say. He mercifully broke the silence.

" 'If you can't tell me what you'd like to be happening,' he said, 'you don't have a problem yet. You're just complaining. A problem only exists if there is a difference between what is *actually* happening and what you *desire* to be happening.'

"Being a quick learner, I suddenly realized I knew what I wanted to be happening. After I told him, he asked me to talk about what may have caused the discrepancy between the actual and the desired.

"After I did that, he said, 'Now, what are you going to do about it?'

" 'Well, I could do A,' I said.

" 'If you did A, would what you want to happen actually happen?' he asked.

" 'No,' I said.

" 'Then you have a lousy solution. What else could you do?' he asked.

" 'I could do B,' I said.

" 'But if you do B, will what you want to happen really happen?' he countered again.

" 'No,' I realized.

" 'Then that's also a bad solution,' he said. 'What else can you do?'

"I thought about it for a couple of minutes and said, 'I could do C. But if I do C, what I want won't happen, so that's not a solution, is it?'

" 'Right. You're starting to come around,' he joked. 'Is there anything else you could do?'

"Feeling relieved, I laughed and said, 'Maybe I could combine some of these solutions.'

" 'That sounds worth trying,' he said.

" 'In fact, if I do A this week, B next week, and C in two weeks, I'll have it solved. That's fantastic. Thanks so much. You solved my problem for me.'

" 'I did not,' he insisted. 'You solved it yourself. I just asked you the kinds of questions you can ask yourself in the future.'

"I knew what he had done, of course. He'd shown me how to solve problems so that I could do it on my own."

"Is that what you mean by seeing what good performance looks like?" the young man asked.

"Yes. My Manager *shows* me how to do it so I can understand it and do it myself.

"Then at the end of the call, he said, 'You're good, Teresa. Remember that the next time you have a problem.'"

Teresa leaned back in her chair and looked as if she were reliving her first encounter with the Manager.

"I remember smiling afterward. I realized what he was doing meant he wouldn't have to participate so much with me in the future."

"That's because you could learn to solve problems better yourself."

"Yes. He wants everyone on our team to enjoy doing our jobs better and sooner."

The young man thought for a moment and said, "I can see how this would make the organization more responsive, with more people on the team able to act on their own.

"Do you mind if I write a brief summary of what I've learned so far?"

Teresa responded, "I think that's a good idea."

Then the young man wrote:

:01® **ONE MINUTE GOALS WORK WELL WHEN YOU:**

1. Plan the goals together and describe them briefly and clearly. Show people what good performance looks like.

2. Have people write out each of their goals, with due dates, on a single page.

3. Ask them to review their most important goals each day, which takes only a few minutes to do.

4. Encourage people to take a minute to look at what they're *doing*, and see if their behavior matches their goals.

5. If it doesn't, encourage them to re-think what they're doing so they can realize their goals sooner.

The young man showed his summary to Teresa.

"That's it!" she said. "You're a fast learner."

"Thank you," he said, feeling good about himself.

"If setting One Minute Goals is the First Secret to becoming a One Minute Manager, can I ask what the other two are?"

Teresa grinned, looked at her watch, and said, "Why don't you ask Paul Trenell? You're scheduled to see him after we finish, aren't you?"

He was impressed that Teresa already knew his schedule. He rose to shake her hand and said, "Yes, and thank you so much for your time."

"You're welcome. Time is one thing I have a lot more of now. As you can probably tell, I'm becoming a New One Minute Manager myself."

"You mean you notice what's changing, and look for new ways to apply the Three Secrets?"

"Yes. Adapting to change is one of my main goals."

A s the young man left Teresa's office, he was struck by the simplicity of what he'd heard. He thought, *It makes sense. After all, how can you be an effective manager unless you and your team are clear about goals and what good performance looks like?*

When he got to Paul Trenell's office, he was surprised to meet someone so young. Paul was in his late twenties or early thirties.

"So you've been to see our Manager. He's quite a guy, isn't he?"

The young man was already getting used to the Manager being called "quite a guy."

"I guess he is."

"Did he tell you about how he manages?"

"He did. Is it true?" asked the young man, wondering if he'd get a different answer from Teresa's.

"It sure is. My boss at the last place I worked was a micromanager, but our New One Minute Manager doesn't believe in that style."

"You mean you don't get help from him?"

"Not as much as I did when I was first learning. He trusts me more now.

"However, he spends a good amount of time with me at the beginning of a new project or responsibility."

"Yes, I just learned about setting One Minute Goals," interjected the young man.

"Actually, I wasn't thinking about One Minute Goals. I was referring to One Minute Praisings."

"One Minute Praisings? Is that the Second Secret?"

"Yes. In fact, when I first started to work here, my Manager made it very clear to me what he was going to do."

"What was that?"

"He said it would be a lot easier for me to do well if he gave me crystal-clear feedback on how I was doing. He said it would help me succeed—that I had talent and he wanted to keep me. He also wanted me to enjoy my work and to be a big help to the organization.

"Then he said he would let me know in *very specific terms* when I was doing well and when I wasn't. He cautioned me that it might not be very comfortable at first for either of us."

"Why?"

"Because, as he pointed out to me then, most managers don't manage that way. He assured me that if succeeding in my job was important to me, I would soon realize that feedback is an invaluable tool."

"Can you give me an example of what you're talking about?"

"Sure," Paul replied. "When I started working here, I noticed that after my Manager and I set our One Minute Goals, he stayed in close contact."

"How did he do that?"

"Two ways. First, he observed my activities. Even if he was far away, he would look at various data that showed how I was doing. Second, he required me to send him reports of my progress."

"How did you feel about that?"

"At first, it was unsettling. Then I recalled that he'd said he would be watching me in the beginning in order to catch me doing something right."

"Catch you doing something *right*?" said the young man.

"Yes. We have a saying around here that every manager lives by."

*

*Help People
Reach Their
Full Potential.*

*Catch Them
Doing Something
Right.*

*

The young man had never heard of a manager doing that, even though he'd met many managers.

Paul continued, "In most organizations the managers spend most of their time catching people doing what?"

The young man smiled knowingly and said, "Doing something wrong."

"Right!" Paul smiled. "No pun intended.

"Here we put the accent on the positive by catching people doing something right, especially as they begin a new task."

The young man made a few notes, then glanced up and asked, "So, what happens when he catches you doing something right?"

"That's when he gives a One Minute Praising," Paul said with delight.

"What does that mean?" the young man asked.

"When he notices you have done something right, he tells you precisely what you did right, and how good he feels about it.

"He pauses for a moment so you can feel it, too. Then he reinforces the praise by encouraging you to keep up the good work."

"I don't think I've ever heard of a manager doing that," the young man said. "That must make you feel pretty good."

"It certainly does, and for several reasons. First, I get a Praising soon after I've done something right." Paul leaned forward and confided, "I don't have to wait for a performance review, if you know what I mean."

"I know," the young man said. "It's awful to have to wait to know how you're doing."

"I agree. Second, since he specifies exactly what I did right, I know he knows what I am doing and is sincere. Third, he is consistent."

"Consistent?" echoed the young man.

"Yes. He praises me when I'm doing my job well and deserve it, even if things are not going well for him personally or here at work. I know he may be annoyed about things happening elsewhere. But he responds to where I am, not just to where he is at the time. I really appreciate that."

"Doesn't all this praising take up a lot of the Manager's time?" the young man asked.

"No. Remember, you don't have to praise someone for very long for that person to know you notice how they're doing. It usually takes less than a minute."

The young man said, "And that's why it's called a One Minute Praising."

"Right," said Paul.

"So is he always trying to catch you doing something right?"

"No, of course not," Paul answered. "It's mostly in the beginning, when you start working here and when you begin a new project or responsibility. After you get to know the ropes, you know he has confidence in you because later on you don't see him that often."

"Really? Isn't that a letdown after all the attention?"

"Not really, because you and he have other ways of knowing when your job performance is praiseworthy. You both can review the data that has been posted— sales figures, expenditures, production schedules, and so on.

"In time," Paul added, "you begin to catch your-self doing things right. You start praising yourself. You wonder when he might praise you again—which he sometimes does—and that keeps you going even when he's not around. It's uncanny. I've never worked so hard at a job in my life. Or enjoyed it so much.

"Here's why: I know when I get a Praising, I've *earned* it. I've seen how it builds confidence, which turns out to be very important."

"Why do you think that's so important?"

"Because confidence that is *earned* helps you deal with all the changes that are occurring. We're expected to be confident enough to innovate in order to stay ahead."

"Is that why your Manager gives you the opportu-nity to solve a problem yourself, rather than participat-ing in your decision?"

"Yes. Plus, it saves a manager time. I do the same with the people on my team, so they, too, become more capable."

"I'm beginning to see a pattern here. You connect One Minute Goals to Praisings, which brings out the best in people."

"Exactly."

"Could you give me a moment to make some notes about how to use One Minute Praisings?"

"Certainly," Paul said.

The young man wrote:

## :01® A ONE MINUTE PRAISING WORKS WELL WHEN YOU:

### THE FIRST HALF-MINUTE

1. Praise people as soon as possible.

2. Let people know what they did right—be specific.

3. Tell people how good you feel about what they did right, and how it helps.

### PAUSE

4. Pause for a moment to allow people time to feel good about what they've done.

### THE SECOND HALF-MINUTE

5. Encourage them to do more of the same.

6. Make it clear you have confidence in them and support their success.

"So, if One Minute Goals and Praisings are the First and Second Secrets, may I ask what the Third Secret is?"

Paul rose from his chair. "Maybe you'd like to ask Jon Levy that. I understand you're planning to talk with him next."

"Yes, I am. I want to thank you so much for your time."

"That's OK. Time is one thing I have more of. You see, I'm becoming a New One Minute Manager myself."

The visitor nodded. This was not the first time he'd heard that in this organization.

He left the building and took a walk among the trees nearby to think about what he was discovering.

He was struck again by the common sense and simplicity of what he had heard. *How can you argue with the effectiveness of catching people doing something right?* the young man thought. *Isn't that what everyone would like to experience?*

*But do One Minute Praisings really work?* he wondered. *Does this One Minute Management stuff really get bottom-line results?*

As he walked along, his curiosity about results increased. So he returned to the Manager's assistant and asked if it would be possible to reschedule his appointment with Jon Levy for sometime the next morning. He explained that before he talked to Jon, he wanted to speak with someone who would have information on all the different divisions in the company.

"Jon says tomorrow morning is fine," Courtney said as she hung up the phone.

Then she called downtown and made the new appointment the young man had requested. He was to see Liz Aquino. Courtney said, "I'm confident she will be able to give you the data you're looking for."

He thanked her and, feeling hungry, went across the street to have something to eat and to prepare for his next meeting.

After lunch, the young man went downtown and met with Liz Aquino. Following a polite discussion about why he was there, he got down to business by asking, "Based on the data you have, what is the best managed of all your operations in the company?"

A moment later he laughed as he heard Liz say, "You won't have to look very far, because it is the New One Minute Manager's. His operation is the most efficient and effective of all of our facilities—and it's been that way for years. No matter how things change, he adapts. He's quite a guy, isn't he?"

"Remarkable," said the young man. "Does he have the best equipment and technology?"

"No," said Liz. "In fact, he's got some of the oldest."

"Well, he can't be perfect," said the young man, still puzzled by the New One Minute Manager's style. "Does he have much turnover?"

"Come to think of it," Liz said, "he does have turnover. People do leave his division."

"Aha," the young man said, thinking he was onto something.

"What happens after they leave the New One Minute Manager?" the young man asked.

"We usually give them their own operation," Liz responded. "He's our best developer of people. Whenever we have an opening and need a good manager, we call him. He always has somebody who is ready."

Fascinated, he thanked Liz for her time—but this time he got a different response.

"I was glad I could fit you in today," she said. "The rest of my week is really jammed. I wish I knew how he continues to do it. I've been meaning to go over there and see him, but I just haven't had time."

Smiling, the young man said, "I'll give you his Secrets as a gift when I find them out myself. Just like he's sharing them with me."

"That would be a precious present," Liz said with a smile. She looked at her cluttered office and sighed. "I could use whatever help I can get."

He left Liz's office and walked out of the building, shaking his head. The Manager was absolutely fascinating to him.

That night the young man had a very restless sleep thinking about the next day—about learning the Third Secret.

The next morning he arrived at Jon Levy's office at the stroke of nine. He got the usual "He's quite a guy, isn't he?" routine, but by now the young man was getting to the point where he could sincerely say, "Yes, he is!"

Jon said, "He's amazing. He's been around for years but he's moved with the times. He keeps things new and fresh. He's evolved and he's sharper than ever.

"One of the most remarkable things he does differently now is how he responds to us when we've done something wrong."

"When you do something wrong? I thought a key motto around here was *Catch People Doing Something Right.*"

"It is," said Jon. "But—

"You need to know I've been working here for a good while and I know this operation inside and out. As a result, my Manager doesn't have to spend much time with me on One Minute Goals or Praisings. In fact, I usually write out my goals before I meet with him. Then we go over them."

"Do you write each goal on a separate page?"

"Yes. No longer than a paragraph or two, which takes only about a minute to review.

"I love my work and I'm good at it. I've learned to give myself Praisings. In fact, I believe if you're not for yourself, who is?" Then he added, "And I'm for *others*, too."

"So, doesn't your Manager praise you?"

"Sometimes. But he doesn't have to very often because I beat him to the punch. When I do something especially good, I might even ask him for a Praising."

"How would you ever have the nerve to do that?" asked the young man.

"It's like making a bet where I either win or break even. If he gives me the Praising, I win. But if he doesn't, I break even. I didn't have it before I asked."

The young man smiled. "I like that idea.

"But what about when something goes wrong?"

"Well, mistakes do happen. If I or someone on my team makes a significant mistake, that's when I may get a One Minute Re-Direct."

"A what?" the young man asked.

"A One Minute Re-Direct. It's the *new* version of the important Third Secret.

"Praising people doesn't always work if it isn't combined with Re-Directs to correct mistakes when they occur.

"While I don't always like someone pointing out my mistakes, a Re-Direct can help me get back on track and achieve my goals. And that helps both me and our organization succeed.

"Back when we were a top-down managed company, this Third Secret was called the One Minute Reprimand, which was remarkably effective for its time. But the New One Minute Manager adapted it when things changed."

"Adapted it?"

"Yes. Today we need to get more done *sooner* with fewer resources. And people want to find more satisfaction and value in their work.

"Now, everybody needs to be a learner because things are changing so much. Even if I'm an expert, the next day my area might be eliminated. A One Minute Re-Direct helps me learn, because it can let me see what I need to do differently."

The visitor asked, "How does it work?"

"It's simple," said Jon.

"I figured you'd say that."

Jon laughed and continued, "If I make a mistake, my Manager is quick to respond."

"What does he do?"

"First, he makes sure he's made the goal we've set clear. If it isn't, he takes responsibility for that, and clarifies the goal.

"Then he provides me with a One Minute Re-Direct in two parts. In the first half he focuses on my mistake. In the second half he focuses on me."

"So when does he do this?"

"As soon as he becomes aware of the mistake. He confirms the facts with me and we review what's gone wrong. He's very specific.

"Then he tells me how he *feels* about the mistake and its possible impact on our results, sometimes in no uncertain terms.

"After he tells me how he feels, he's quiet for a few seconds to let it sink in. That quiet pause turns out to be surprisingly important."

"Why?"

"Because a quiet moment gives me time to feel concerned about my mistake and think about the impact it might have on me and the organization."

"How long is he quiet?"

"Only a few seconds, but sometimes it seems longer when you're on the receiving end."

Jon continued. "In the second part of the Re-Direct, he reminds me that I'm better than my mistake and that he has confidence and trust in me. He says he doesn't expect a repeat of that mistake and looks forward to working with me."

"It sounds to me that the Re-Direct makes you think twice about what you've done."

Jon nodded. "It does."

"Could you tell me more about the key parts of using a One Minute Re-Direct?"

"Sure. He specifies exactly what went wrong so I know that he's on top of things and that he doesn't want me or my team to be known for poor or mediocre work.

"Since he ends the Re-Direct by reaffirming that he values me and my team, it's easier for me not to react negatively and become defensive. I don't try to rationalize away my mistake by fixing blame on somebody else.

"Of course, it helps to know that he will take responsibility if a goal isn't clear to everyone. Because of that, I know he's being fair.

"The Re-Direct only takes about a minute, and when it's over, it's over. But you remember it, and since it ends in a supportive way, you want to get back on track."

"I know what you're talking about," the young man said. "I'm afraid I asked him—"

Jon interrupted, "I hope you didn't ask him to make a decision for you."

The young man was embarrassed. "I did."

Jon chuckled. "Then you know a little about what it's like to be on the receiving end of a One Minute Re-Direct, although I suspect you got a mild one.

"Around here we're aware that if you are new to our company's culture but you need a Re-Direct, it should be a mild one so you don't get discouraged. Our goal is to build confidence in people to help us get better results."

"It may have been a mild one," the young man said, "but I don't think I'll ask him to make a decision for me again."

Then he asked, "Does he ever make a mistake? He seems almost too perfect."

Jon laughed. "Of course he makes mistakes. He's human. But he's the first to acknowledge it.

"In fact, he even encourages us to speak up if we notice he may be mistaken about something. It doesn't happen often, but he says it helps him prevent an error he might make in the future. It's one of the many reasons we like working with him.

"He can be gruff sometimes, but he has a good sense of humor, and that helps.

"For example, he's really good at catching a mistake I've made, but sometimes he forgets to give me the second half of the Re-Direct."

"The part where he thinks well of you as a person?"

"Yes. When he forgets, I point it out to him and kid him about it."

"You really do that?"

"Well, I might first take some time to understand what I did wrong and think about what I need to change.

"Just the other day I phoned him to say I knew I was wrong and wouldn't let it happen again. Then I laughed and said I'd really like to get the reaffirming part of the Re-Direct, which he forgot to do, so I could feel better."

"And what did *he* do?"

"He laughed, then apologized and said he meant to say he still has confidence and trust in me. When we hung up, I did feel better."

"That amazes me," the young man said.

"Yes, when he keeps his sense of humor, it helps him and everyone around him. He's taught us to laugh at ourselves when we make a mistake, and get over it by doing better work."

"Wow! So how did you learn to do that?"

"By watching *him* do it."

The young man was beginning to realize how valuable such a manager could be.

"I notice the Third Secret continues a pattern in this One Minute system of leading and managing. Goals make clear what is most important to focus on, Praisings build confidence that helps you succeed, and Re-Directs address mistakes. And all three of these help people feel better about themselves and produce good results.

"Why does using a combination of Goals, Praisings, and Re-Directs work so well?"

"I'll let you ask our New One Minute Manager that," Jon said as he rose from his chair and walked him to the door.

The young man thanked him for his time.

Jon smiled. "You already know what my response to the subject of time is going to be."

They both laughed. The young man was beginning to feel like an insider rather than a visitor, and it felt good.

As soon as he was in the hall, the young man realized how much information Jon had given him in the little time they'd spent together.

He made notes to remind himself how to use a One Minute Re-Direct when a person has made a mistake.

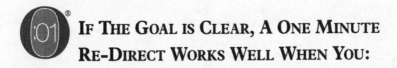

## IF THE GOAL IS CLEAR, A ONE MINUTE RE-DIRECT WORKS WELL WHEN YOU:

### THE FIRST HALF-MINUTE

1. Re-Direct people as soon as possible.

2. Confirm the facts first, and review the mistake together—be specific.

3. Express how you *feel* about the mistake and its impact on results.

### PAUSE

4. Be quiet for a moment to allow people time to feel concerned about what they've done.

### THE SECOND HALF-MINUTE

5. Remember to let them know that they're better than their mistake, and that you think well of them as a person.

6. Remind them that you have confidence and trust in them, and support their success.

7. Realize that when the Re-Direct is over, it's over.

The young man may not have believed in the effectiveness of the One Minute Re-Direct if he hadn't personally experienced its effect. Even though he knew he got a mild one, he also knew he did not look forward to another one.

However, everyone makes mistakes, and he knew if he ever worked for such a manager and made a major mistake, he probably would get a much stronger Re-Direct. But it didn't worry him. He knew it would be fair.

As he headed back toward the Manager's office, he kept thinking about the surprising power of One Minute Management, and how it had been improved for a changing world.

All three of the Secrets seemed to make sense. *But why do they work?* he wondered.

*And why is the New One Minute Manager still the most productive and admired manager in the company?*

When he arrived at the Manager's office, Courtney said, "He's been wondering when you'd be back to see him."

As the young man entered the office, he noticed again how clear and uncluttered it was.

The Manager greeted him with a warm smile. "What did you find out in your travels?"

"A great deal!"

"Tell me what you discovered."

"I found out why you're called the New One Minute Manager. It's because you keep adapting your Three Secrets. You and your team set One Minute Goals together to make sure everyone knows what they're being held accountable for and what good performance looks like.

"Then you catch people doing something right and give them a One Minute Praising.

"And when you notice people have made a mistake, you provide them with a One Minute Re-Direct."

"What do you think about all that?"

"I'm surprised at how little time it takes, and yet it seems to work."

The young man hesitated and then said, "I hope I'm not being rude with this question, but do you really think it takes only a minute to do all the things you need to do as a manager?"

The Manager laughed. "Of course not. But it's a way to make a complicated job more manageable. It often takes only a minute to refocus on goals and give people important feedback on how they're doing.

"Using the Three Secrets probably represents only 20% of the activities we engage in, yet they help us achieve 80% of the outcome we're looking for. It's the old 80/20 law."

The Manager added, "What else have you noticed?"

"Well, people obviously enjoy working here and you collaborate with each other to get great results. I'm convinced it works for you."

The Manager assured him, "And if you do it, it will work for you, too."

"Perhaps, but I think I would be more likely to do it if I could understand more about *why* it works."

"Sure. That's true of everyone, young man. The more we understand *why* something works, the more apt we are to use it.

"Let me show you one of the reminders I keep on my computer."

The young man turned and saw:

*

***The Best
Minute
I Spend
Is The One
I Invest
In People.***

*

"It's ironic that most companies spend so much of their money on people's salaries, and yet they spend only a small fraction of their budget to develop people. In fact, most companies spend more time and money on maintaining their buildings, technology, and equipment than they do on developing people."

"I never thought of that," the young man admitted. "But if it's the people who get the results, then it makes good sense to invest more in people."

"Exactly." The Manager then revealed, "I wish I'd had someone invest in me sooner when I first went to work."

"What do you mean?" the young man asked.

"With most of the organizations I worked in, I often didn't know what I was supposed to be doing. No one bothered to tell me. If you asked me whether I was doing a good job, I would say either 'I don't know' or 'I think so.' If you asked why I thought so, I would reply, 'I haven't been chewed out by my boss lately' or 'No news is good news.' It was almost as if my main motivation was to avoid punishment."

The young man said, "I can see why you manage differently. But I still wonder why the Three Secrets are so effective.

"For example, why does setting One Minute Goals work?"

"You want to know why setting One Minute Goals works," the Manager echoed. "Fine." He got up and began to pace slowly around the room.

"Let me give you an analogy that might help. I've seen a lot of unmotivated people at work in the various organizations I've been employed in over the years. But I haven't seen that many unmotivated people after work.

"One night, years ago, I was bowling and I saw some of the 'problem employees' from my previous organization. One of the real problem people, who I remembered all too well, approached the line and rolled the bowling ball. Soon he started to hoot and holler and jump around. Why do you think he was so happy?"

"Because he knocked down all the pins."

"Exactly. Why do you think he and other people don't have that same level of excitement at work?"

The young man gave it some thought. "Because they don't know where the pins are—what they're aiming at. I get it. How long would they want to bowl if they couldn't see the pins?"

"Right," said the One Minute Manager. "I believe many managers assume wrongly that the people on their team know what to aim for.

"When you assume that people know what's expected of them, you are creating an ineffective form of bowling. You put the pins up, but when the bowler goes to roll the ball, he notices there is a sheet across the pins. So when he rolls the ball and it slips under the sheet, he hears a crack but doesn't know how many pins he knocked down. When you ask him how he did, he says 'I don't know. But it felt good.'

"It's like playing golf at night. A lot of my friends have given up golf, and when I asked them why, they said, 'Because the courses are too crowded.'

"When I suggested they play at night, they laughed, because who would ever play golf without being able to see where to hit the ball?

"It's the same with watching team sports. How many people would watch two teams compete if there was no way to score?"

"Yeah. Why is that?" asked the young man.

"It's all because the number one motivator of people is feedback on results. They want to know how they're doing.

"In fact, we have another saying here that's worth noting: *Feedback Is the Breakfast of Champions*. It's feedback that keeps us going.

"Unfortunately, even when some managers learn that feedback on results is the number one motivator of people, they usually set up a third form of bowling.

"When the bowler goes to the line to roll the ball, the pins are still up and the sheet is in place but now there is another ingredient in the game—a supervisor standing behind the sheet. When the bowler rolls the ball, he hears the crash of falling pins, and the supervisor holds up two fingers to signify he knocked down two pins. Actually, do most managers say, 'You got two'?"

"No," the young man said with a smile. "They usually say, 'You missed eight.'"

"That's right! The question I always used to ask was, 'Why doesn't the manager "lift up the sheet" so both of you can see the pins?' The answer was that he had the great business tradition of performance review coming up."

"Because he had performance review coming up?" wondered the young man aloud.

"Why is it," the Manager asked, "that most people don't know how they're doing until they go through their performance review, and learn all the things they didn't do right?

"Then when the person is told they are not up for a bonus or a promotion, how does that person feel? How long will it be before they start wishing they worked somewhere else?"

"I know the answer. One minute!" the young man joked.

The Manager laughed.

"Why do you suppose managers would put someone through that?" asked the young man.

"So they can look good," said the Manager.

"What do you mean?"

"How do you think you would be viewed by your boss if you rated everyone that reported to you at the highest level on your performance review scale?"

"Probably as a soft touch—someone who can't discriminate between good performance and poor performance."

"Precisely," said the Manager. "In order to look good as a manager in most organizations, you have to catch some of your people doing things wrong. You have to have a few winners, a few losers, and everyone else somewhere in the middle.

"I remember one time when visiting my son's school, I observed a fifth-grade teacher giving a geography test to her class. When I asked her why she didn't allow the kids to use maps during the test, she said, 'I couldn't do that because all the kids would get 100%.' As though it would be bad for everyone to do well and get an A.

"Everyone might not do a great job of using the resources at hand, so they may not get an A, but why not set it up so that everyone has a chance to be a winner?"

The Manager continued, "I remember once reading that back when practically everyone knew their own phone number, someone asked the genius Albert Einstein what his number was and he went to the phone book to look it up.

"He said he never cluttered his mind with information he could find somewhere else.

"Now, if you didn't know better, what would you think of someone in those days who had to look up his own number? Would you think he was a winner or a loser?"

The young man grinned and said, "Probably a loser."

"Sure," the Manager responded. "I would, too. But we'd both be wrong, wouldn't we?"

The young man nodded his agreement.

"It's easy for any of us to make this mistake," the Manager said. Then he showed his visitor something on his computer. "Look at this."

\*

*Everyone*
*Is A Potential Winner.*

*Some People*
*Are Disguised*
*As Losers.*

*Don't Let*
*Their Appearances*
*Fool You.*

\*

"You see," the Manager said, "you really have three choices as a manager. First, you can hire winners. They are hard to find and they cost money. Or, second, if you can't find a winner, you can hire someone with the potential to be a winner. Then you systematically help that person become a winner.

"If you are not willing to do either of the first two—and I am continually amazed at the number of managers who won't spend the money to hire a winner or take the time to develop someone to become a winner—then there is only the third choice left: prayer."

That stopped the young man cold. "Prayer?"

The Manager laughed quietly. "That's just my attempt at humor, young man. But when you think about it, there are many managers who are saying this prayer daily: 'Please let this person work out.'"

The young man laughed and said, "If you hire a winner, it's really easy to be a One Minute Manager, isn't it?"

"Sure," said the Manager with a smile. "All you have to do with people who are winners is set One Minute Goals and let them run with the ball."

"I understand from Jon Levy you almost don't even have to do that with him."

"You're right," said the Manager. "He's forgotten more than most people know around here. But with everyone, winner or potential winner, setting strategic One Minute Goals is a basic tool for productive behavior."

"Is it true that no matter who initiates setting the One Minute Goals," the young man asked, "each goal always needs to be described on one page, including due dates?"

"Yes, it's true."

"Why is that?"

"So people can quickly review their goals daily and check their performance against those goals."

"I understand you have them write down only their major goals and responsibilities and not every aspect of their job," the young man said.

"Yes. That's because I don't want a lot of goals filed away somewhere and looked at only once a year when it's time for a performance review or setting next year's goals.

"As you might have seen, people on our team keep this valuable reminder nearby." He handed him a card that read:

★

**Take a Minute To**
*Look At Your Goals.*

**Then Look At What**
**You're Doing**

*And See If It Matches*
*Your Goals.*

★

The young man was amazed at the powerful simplicity of those words.

"Could I get a copy of that?" he asked.

"Sure," the Manager said.

As he was taking notes on what he was learning, the aspiring young manager said, "You know, it's difficult to grasp everything there is to learn about One Minute Management in such a short time.

"There's certainly more I'd like to learn about One Minute Goals, but could we move on to discuss One Minute Praisings?"

"Sure. You're probably wondering why they work, too."

"Well, I think everyone likes to be praised. But after a while don't people start to feel like the Praisings are fake?"

The Manager responded, "That depends on whether the Praising is merited and sincere."

"Let's look at a few examples. Maybe then it will be clear to you why One Minute Praisings work so well."

"I'd like that," said the young man.

"One example is when parents first help children learn to walk. Can you imagine standing a child up and saying, 'Walk,' and when he falls down you pick him up and spank him and say, 'I told you to walk'?

"Instead, you stand the child up and the first day he wobbles a little bit, and you get all excited and say, 'He stood, he stood!' and you hug and kiss the child. The next day he stands for a moment and maybe wobbles a step, and you are all over him with kisses and hugs.

"Finally, the child, realizing that this is a pretty good deal, starts to stand on his legs more and more until he eventually walks.

"The same thing goes for teaching a child to speak. Suppose you wanted a child to say, 'Give me a glass of water, please.' If you waited until the child said the whole sentence before you gave her any water, the child would die of thirst.

"So you start off by saying, 'Water, water.' All of a sudden one day the child says, 'Waller.' You jump all over the place, hug and kiss the child, and get Grandmother on the phone so the child can say, 'Waller, waller.' That wasn't 'water,' but it was close.

"Now, you don't want a kid going into a restaurant at the age of twenty-one asking for a glass of 'waller,' so after a while you only accept the word 'water' and then you begin on 'please.'

"These examples illustrate that the most important—and natural—thing to do to help people become winners is to catch them doing something *approximately* right in the beginning. Then you move on toward the desired result."

"So the key in the beginning," the young man said, "is to catch somebody doing something approximately right until they can eventually learn to do it right."

"You've got it," said the Manager. "By setting up a series of goals, they are establishing targets that can be more easily achieved.

"At work, and in life, too, you don't have to catch a winner doing things right very often, because good performers catch *themselves* doing things right. But people who are learning benefit from praise and encouragement from others."

The young man asked, "Is that why you observe new people a lot in the beginning, or when your more experienced people are starting a new project?"

"Yes. Most managers wait until people do something exactly right before they praise them. As a result, many people never get to become high performers because their managers concentrate on catching them doing things wrong—that is, anything that falls short of the final desired performance."

"That doesn't sound like it would be very effective," the young man suggested.

"It isn't," said the Manager.

"Sadly, that is what too many organizations do with new, inexperienced people. They welcome them aboard, take them around to meet everybody, and then leave them alone. Not only do they not catch the new people doing anything approximately right, but periodically they zap them just to keep them moving.

"This has been a popular management style for a long time. I call it the leave-alone-zap style. You leave a person alone, expecting good performance from them, and when you don't get it, you zap them."

"What happens to these people?" asked the young man.

"If you've been in any organization, and I understand you've visited many, you know because you've seen them. They do as little as possible."

The young man laughed. "You're right. I've seen it." Then he added, "Working with that kind of a manager, you can understand why so many people don't enjoy their work."

The Manager agreed. "That's so true. And they're also not engaged in what they're doing or very interested in doing good work."

The young man said, "I'm beginning to see why the One Minute Praising seems to work so well. It's certainly better than focusing only on what's wrong."

Then he added, "It's funny, but that reminds me of some friends of mine. They told me they had a new pet, and asked what I thought of their great idea for house-training the dog."

"I'm almost afraid to ask," said the Manager. "How were they going to do it?"

"They said if the dog had an accident on the rug, they were going to take the dog, shove his nose in it, pound him on the butt with a newspaper, and throw the dog out the open kitchen window into the backyard—where the dog was supposed to do his job."

The Manager laughed.

"Then they asked me what I thought would happen with this method. I laughed, because I knew what would happen—and it did.

"After about three days, the dog pooped on the floor and jumped out the window. The dog didn't know what to do, but he knew he had better clear the area."

The Manager roared his approval.

"That's a great story. Punishment doesn't work when you use it with someone who's learning.

"Rather than punish inexperienced people who are still learning, we need to re-direct them. That involves resetting clear One Minute Goals to make sure they understand what's expected of them and what good performance looks like."

The young man asked, "So, after you have done that, do you try to catch them doing something approximately right again?"

"Precisely. In the beginning you're always trying to notice situations where you can give a legitimate One Minute Praising."

Then, looking the young man straight in the eye, the Manager said, "You are a very enthusiastic and receptive learner. That makes me feel good about sharing the Secrets of One Minute Management with you."

They both smiled. They knew a One Minute Praising when they heard one.

"I'd rather have a Praising than a Re-Direct," the young man said. "I understand now why One Minute Goals and Praisings work. They make good sense.

"But why do One Minute Re-Directs work?"

The Manager explained, "There are several reasons why One Minute Re-Directs work so well.

"To begin with, the feedback happens in small doses, because you catch the mistake early on.

"Many managers gunnysack their feedback. That is, they store up observations of poor behavior until frustration builds.

"When performance review time comes, these managers are angry in general because their sack is really full. So they charge in and dump it all at one time.

"They tell people every single thing they have done wrong for the last several weeks or months or more.

"It's not fair to people to save up negative feelings about their poor performance, and it's not effective."

The young man breathed a deep sigh. "So true. And that often happens at home, too."

"Yes, some parents and spouses do that, too, and they get the same poor results.

"What happens then is people usually end up disagreeing about the facts, or they simply keep quiet and become resentful. Often, the person receiving the feedback becomes defensive. They don't own what they have done wrong.

"This is another version of the leave-alone-zap way of communicating.

"If managers would address things earlier, they could deal with one behavior at a time and the person would not be overwhelmed. They'd be more likely to hear the feedback the way it was intended. That's why I think performance review should be an ongoing process, not something you do only once a year."

"So is that why the Re-Direct works? Because the manager deals fairly and clearly with one behavior at a time, so the person receiving the feedback can hear it?"

"Yes. You want to get rid of the bad behavior but keep the good person, so you don't attack the person just because they've made a mistake."

"Is that why you make it a point to praise people in the second half of the Re-Direct?"

"Yes. The goal is not to tear people down, but to build them up.

"When our self-concept is under attack, we feel a need to defend ourselves and our actions, even to the extent of distorting the facts. When people become defensive, they don't learn.

"So you want to separate their behavior from their worth. Reaffirming them after you've addressed the mistake focuses on their behavior without attacking them personally.

"When you walk away, you want the person aware of and concerned about what they did, instead of turning to a coworker and talking about how they were mistreated or what they think of your leadership style.

"Otherwise, the person takes no responsibility for the mistake and the manager becomes the villain."

The young man asked, "Why wouldn't you give the Praising part of the Re-Direct first and then the critique?"

"For some reason, it just doesn't work that way. Some people, now that I think of it, say that I am nice and tough as a manager. But to be more accurate, I'm actually tough and nice."

"Tough and nice?" echoed the young man.

"Yes. In that order. This is an old philosophy that has worked well for literally thousands of years. There's a story from ancient China that illustrates this.

"Once upon a time, an emperor appointed a second-in-command. He called him the prime minister and, in effect, said to him, 'Why don't we divide up the tasks? Why don't you do all the punishing and I'll do all the rewarding?' The prime minister said, 'Fine. I'll do all the punishing and you do all the rewarding.'"

"I think I'm going to like this story," the young man said.

"You will," the Manager said with a knowing smile.

"Now, this emperor soon noticed that whenever he asked someone to do something, they might do it or they might not do it. However, when the prime minister spoke, people moved.

"So the emperor called the prime minister back in and said, 'Why don't we divide the tasks again? You have been doing all the punishing here for quite a while. Now let me do the punishing and you do the rewarding.' So the prime minister and the emperor switched roles.

"Within a month there was a revolt. The emperor had been a nice person, rewarding and being kind to everyone; then he started to punish people. People said, 'What's wrong with that old codger?' and they threw him out on his ear.

"When they came to look for a replacement, they said, 'You know who's really starting to come around now? The prime minister.' So they made him emperor."

"Is that a true story?" the young man asked.

"Who knows?" the Manager said with a laugh. "Seriously," he added, "I do know this: if you are first tough on the behavior, and *then* supportive of the person, it works better."

"Do you have any modern-day examples of where a One Minute Re-Direct has worked, maybe outside the business world?"

"Sure. Athletic coaches all over the country use the equivalent of a Re-Direct to improve their athletes' performances. For example, a well-known college basketball coach told me he uses it to create championship teams."

"How so?"

"He told me about a time when his best player was playing so poorly in an important game that unless he quickly improved his game, the team would probably lose. So he took this player out of the game and had him sit on the bench."

"His *best* player?" asked the young man.

"How could he afford to take him out of an important game?"

"He couldn't afford *not* to. Unless the player played his A game, the team wasn't going to win and would miss competing in the championship.

"So as the player sat on the bench, this coach told him exactly what he was doing wrong. 'You're missing easy shots, you're not grabbing any rebounds, and you're loafing on defense. I'm angry with you because you don't look like you're even trying!'

"He waited a moment, then added, 'You're better than that. You need to sit on the bench until you're ready to play the way you're capable of.'

"After what seemed like forever, the player stood up, went over to the coach, and said, 'I'm ready to go in, Coach.'

"The coach responded, 'Then get back in there and show me what you can do.'

"When the player got back in, he was all over the court, diving for loose balls, grabbing rebounds, and making his usual shots. Thanks to his effort, the rest of the team also improved their play and they won the game."

"So basically," the young man said, "the coach did the three things that Jon Levy told me about earlier: tell people what they did wrong; tell them how you feel about it; and remind them they are better than that.

"In other words, their performance is bad, but *they* are good."

"Precisely. You see, it is very important when you are leading people to remember that behavior and worth are not the same things. What is really worthwhile is the *person* who's managing their own behavior.

"It applies equally to us when we're managing our *own* behavior.

"In fact, if you realize this," the Manager said as he brought up another screen on his computer, "you will know the key to providing a really successful Re-Direct."

\*

*We Are Not Just*

*Our Behavior.*

*We Are The Person*

*Managing*

*Our Behavior.*

\*

The young man said, "It sounds like there's respect and caring behind a Re-Direct."

"I'm glad you noticed that, young man. You'll be more successful when you respect the individual you're re-directing."

The young man was hesitant to ask the next question. "While One Minute Praisings and One Minute Re-Directs are effective, could they be seen as ways to manipulate people and get them to do what you want?"

"That's a great question. Manipulation involves deceptively controlling people for your own advantage. If you're trying to manipulate people, you're doing a poor job, and it will come back to bite you.

"Your job is to show people how to manage themselves and enjoy it. You want them to succeed when you're not around.

"That is why it is so important to let people know up front what you are doing and why.

"It's like anything else in life. There are things that work and things that don't work. Being honest with people works better. As you may have noticed, being dishonest eventually leads to failing with people."

"I can see now," the young man said, "where the power of your management style comes from—you care about people."

"Yes, I do. And I also care about results!"

The young man was beginning to see more clearly how closely related people and results were.

He remembered how gruff he thought this special Manager was when he first met him.

It was as though the Manager could read his mind. "Sometimes," he said, "you have to care enough to be tough—that is, tough on the poor performance but not on the person.

"As you undoubtedly know, making mistakes is not the problem. It's not learning from them that causes real problems."

The young man asked, "What happens when a person keeps making similar mistakes, after you've already provided them with a Re-Direct?"

"Well, let me ask you, how do you think a manager feels when that happens?"

"Probably unhappy, annoyed, or even angry."

"Yes. That's when you need to take a break and calmly look at the situation, so your emotions don't cause *you* to make a mistake.

"A One Minute Re-Direct is intended to help people learn. However, when a person has learned something and has shown they *can do* it, but they have a *won't do* attitude, you need to look at the cost to the organization, and whether you can afford to keep such a person on the team."

That made sense to the young man.

By now he had grown to like the New One Minute Manager, and knew why people enjoyed working there. They worked *with* him, not *for* him.

The young man said, "Maybe you would find this interesting. I wrote this to remind me of how goals and consequences are related and how One Minute Goals, Praisings, and Re-Directs work together." He showed him a page from his notes:

*

Goals
Begin
Behaviors.

Consequences
Influence
Future Behaviors.

*

"That's good!" the Manager said.

"Do you think so?" the young man asked, wanting to hear the compliment again.

"Young man," the Manager said lightheartedly, "it is not my role in life to be a human tape recorder. I do not have time to repeat myself."

Just when the young man thought he might be praised again, he felt he was in for another One Minute Re-Direct.

But the bright young man kept a straight face and said simply, "What?"

They looked at each other for a moment and then both broke into laughter.

"I like you, young man," the Manager said. "How would you like to work here?"

The young man stared in amazement. "You mean work for you?" he asked enthusiastically.

"No. I mean work for *yourself*, like the other people on our team. I don't believe anybody ever really works for anybody else. Deep down, people like to work for themselves.

"The people on our team work as partners and together we look for ways to improve. I do my best to help them work better, and in the process we all enjoy our work and lives more. And we're a great benefit to our organization."

This was, of course, what the young man had been looking for all along.

"I'd love to work here," he said.

And so he did.

Over time, he benefited greatly from working with such an innovative manager.

And eventually, the inevitable happened.

# H e, too, became a New One Minute Manager.

He became one, not because he thought like one, or talked like one, but because he led and managed like one.

He kept things simple.

He set One Minute Goals.

He gave One Minute Praisings.

He provided One Minute Re-Directs.

He asked brief, important questions; spoke the simple truth; laughed, worked, and enjoyed.

And perhaps most important of all, he not only managed, he also led people to be creative and do new things. He encouraged those around him to do the same for the people they worked with.

He even created a pocket-sized Game Plan to make it easier for people to become a New One Minute Manager. He gave it as a useful gift to those who could benefit from it.

It read:

# The New One Minute Manager's Game Plan

**Start**
Let people know up front what you are going to do to help them win.

**ONE MINUTE GOALS**

- Make it clear what the goals are.
- Show what good behavior looks like.
- Put each goal on one page.
- Quickly review goals frequently.
- Encourage people to notice what they're doing, and see if it matches their goals.
- If not, urge them to change what they're doing and win.

Goals Achieved
(or any part of the goals)

**You Win!**

Goals *Not* Achieved

**You Lose**

To Help You Win

**ONE MINUTE PRAISINGS**

- Praise the behavior.
- Do it soon. Be specific.
- Say how good you feel about it.
- Pause to let people feel good too.
- Encourage them to keep up the good work.

**ONE MINUTE RE-DIRECTS**

- Re-clarify & agree on goals.
- Confirm what happened.
- Describe the mistake soon.
- Say how concerned you feel.
- Pause to let people feel their own concern.
- Tell them they're better than the mistake & you value them.
- When it's over, it's over.

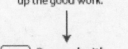

**Proceed with More Success**

**Proceed to Better Performance**

Many years later, he looked back on the time when he first heard about One Minute Management. It seemed like long ago.

The need for his organization to be more agile and responsive had become even greater since he'd first met the New One Minute Manager. So he was very grateful that the special manager had been so generous with his time and knowledge. It had proved to be very valuable.

Remembering his promise to share what he'd learned with others, he had expanded the notes he'd taken long ago and had given a copy to each person on his team.

They'd read it and said that using the Three Secrets had made a real difference.

They found that Praisings, especially when they were balanced with effective Re-Directs, were a powerful way to accomplish Goals sooner.

Several people also revealed they were using the principles at home and were enjoying catching each other doing something right.

Liz Aquino had come by to say, "Thank you for letting me know about the Three Secrets. I have much more time now."

He'd responded, "We have the New One Minute Manager to thank for that."

Sitting at his desk, he realized how fortunate he was.

He now had time to think and plan, and to give his organization the kind of help it really needed.

He had more time to spend with his family and pursue other interests. He even had time to relax. He felt lucky to have less stress than other managers might experience.

Because the people on his team were doing so well, his division had fewer costly personnel problems, less illness, and less absenteeism.

As he looked back, he was glad he hadn't waited to start using One Minute Management until he thought he could do it *just right.*

He'd admitted to his team, "I'm not used to telling people how good they are or how I feel. And I'm not sure I can always remember to tell you that I value and think well of you when I give a Re-Direct."

So, he had to smile when someone said, "Well, you could at least give it a *try!*"

By simply asking people if they wanted to be managed by such a manager, and admitting that he might not always be able to do it right, he'd accomplished something important.

People knew up front that he was honestly on their side from the start, and *that* made all the difference.

H e was lost in thought, so when the phone rang, it startled him.

He heard his assistant say, "Good morning. There is a young woman on the phone who would like to know if she could come and talk with you about the way we manage here."

He smiled, remembering his own early experiences. "I'd be happy to talk with her," he replied.

Later, when he met with the bright young woman, he said, "I'm honored to share what I've learned about leading and managing."

As he offered her a seat he added, "I will only make one request of you."

"What is that?" the visitor asked.

"Simply," he began, "that if you find it useful, you will . . ."

★

*Share It With Others.*

★

the end

# :01 Acknowledgments

Over the years we have learned from and been influenced by many individuals. We would like to acknowledge and give a public praising to:

*Larry Hughes* for his unique, creative publishing of the original edition.

*Drs. Gerald Nelson* and *Richard Levak,* for the One Minute Scolding, an amazingly effective method of parental discipline. We've adapted their method into the One Minute Re-Direct.

*Dr. Elliott Carlisle* for what he taught us about effective delegation.

*Dr. Thomas Connellan* for what he taught us about making behavioral concepts and theories clear and understandable to all.

*Dr. Paul Hersey* for what he taught us about applying insights from the behavioral sciences.

*Dr. Dorothy Jongeward, Jay Shelov,* and *Abe Wagner* for what they taught us about communication and the OK-ness of people.

*Dr. Robert Lorber* for what he taught us about managing consequences in business and industry.

*Dr. Kenneth Majer* for what he taught us about goal setting and performance.

*Dr. Carl Rogers* for what he taught us about personal honesty and openness.

*Louis Tice* for what he taught us about unlocking human potential.

We also want to thank our marvelous literary agent *Margret McBride*; *Richard Andrews*; our excellent editors *Nancy Casey* and *Martha Lawrence*; our talented designer *Patrick Piña*, and *Faye Atchison* for all their help.

# **About the Authors**

**K**en Blanchard, one of the most influential leadership experts in the world, is the coauthor of the iconic bestseller, *The One Minute Manager*, and 60 other books whose combined sales total more than 21 million copies. His groundbreaking works have been translated into more than 42 languages and in 2005 he was inducted into Amazon's Hall of Fame as one of the top 25 bestselling authors of all time.

He is also the cofounder with his wife, Margie, of The Ken Blanchard Companies®, an international management training and consulting firm in San Diego, California, and Lead Like Jesus, a worldwide organization committed to helping people become servant leaders.

Ken has received numerous awards and honors for his contributions in the fields of management, leadership, and speaking. The National Speakers Association awarded him its highest honor, the Council of Peers Award of Excellence. He was inducted into the HRD Hall of Fame by *Training* magazine and he received the Golden Gavel Award from Toastmasters International. Ken also received the Thought Leadership Award by ISA–the Association of Learning Providers.

When he's not writing or speaking, Ken teaches students in the Master of Science in Executive Leadership Program at the University of San Diego.

Born in New Jersey and raised in New York, Ken received an MA degree from Colgate University and a BA and PhD from Cornell University.

**Spencer Johnson, MD,** is one of the most admired thought leaders and widely read authors in the world. His books have become embedded in our language and culture.

Called "The King of Parables" by *USA Today*, Dr. Johnson is often referred to as the best there is at taking complex subjects and presenting simple solutions that work. His brief books contain valuable insights and practical tools that millions of people use to enjoy more happiness and success with less stress.

His thirteen New York Times bestsellers include the #1 titles *Who Moved My Cheese? An A-Mazing Way to Deal with Change* and *The One Minute Manager: The World's Most Popular Way to Manage Your Work and Life*, coauthored with Ken Blanchard.

In a time when many have learned to be skeptical of simplistic answers, millions of readers around the world have found the simple truths in Spencer Johnson's parables to be invaluable.

Dr. Johnson's education includes a BA degree in Psychology from the University of Southern California, an MD degree from the Royal College of Surgeons, and medical clerkships at the Mayo Clinic and Harvard Medical School.

He has served as Research Physician at the Institute for Interdisciplinary Studies; Leadership Fellow at the Harvard Business School, and Adviser to the Center for Public Leadership at Harvard's Kennedy School of Government.

Over 50 million copies of Spencer Johnson's books are in use worldwide in 47 languages.

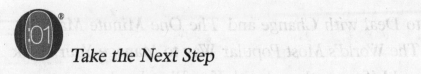

## Take the Next Step

*Available from The Ken Blanchard Companies*

**New One Minute Manager Training**

*The One Minute Manager* has been part of every manager's essential library for over three decades. Now you can develop your management potential by exploring the wisdom of *The New One Minute Manager* and building the practical skills critical to your success. Learn how you can become a more effective manager at kenblanchard.com.

The concepts in this book are some of the many ways that The Ken Blanchard Companies® helps organizations improve performance, employee engagement, and customer loyalty around the world. If you would like additional information about how to experience these benefits within your organization, contact us at:

The Ken Blanchard Companies
The Leadership Difference®
Phone: +1-760-489-5005
Contact: kenblanchard.com/inquire
Website: www.kenblanchard.com

*Available from Spencer Johnson, MD*

**Spencer Johnson's Books**
You may discover more about Dr. Spencer
Johnson's books at www.spencerjohnson.com.

# HARPER LUXE

## THE NEW LUXURY IN READING

We hope you enjoyed reading
our new, comfortable print size and found it
an experience you would like to repeat.

**Well – you're in luck!**

HarperLuxe offers the finest in fiction and
nonfiction books in this same larger print size and
paperback format. Light and easy to read, HarperLuxe
paperbacks are for book lovers who want to see
what they are reading without the strain.

For a full listing of titles and
new releases to come, please visit our website:

**www.HarperLuxe.com**